LIFE AND MIRACLES

OF

ST. BENEDICT

(BOOK TWO OF THE DIALOGUES)

by

Pope St. Gregory the Great

Translated by

ODO J. ZIMMERMANN, O.S.B.

and

BENEDICT R. AVERY, O.S.B.

THE LITURGICAL PRESS
Collegeville, Minnesota

Published with ecclesiastical approval by Liturgical Press, Collegeville, Minnesota.

Printed in the United States of America.

ISBN 13: 978-0-8146-0321-5

ISBN 10: 0-8146-0321-1

INTRODUCTION

There are four books in the *Dialogues*[1] of
St. Gregory the Great (540?-604). The first
three contain accounts of the lives and miracles of various Italian saints, and the fourth
an essay on the immortality of the soul. The
entire second book is devoted to the *Life and
Miracles of St. Benedict*—an emphasis readily
understood in the light of the author's back-
ground and career.

When he was about thirty-five years old,
St. Gregory resigned from the high political
office he held as Prefect of Rome to enter the
religious life. He founded six monasteries on
his estates in Sicily and turned his own home
on the Caelian Hill in Rome into the Monastery of St. Andrew. Then, after distributing
the rest of his wealth among the poor, he entered St. Andrew's as an ordinary monk and
lived there under the Rule of St. Benedict,
which he was later to praise for its discretion.[2]

In 578 Pope Benedict I ordained him one of
the seven deacons of Rome, and the next year
Pope Pelagius II sent him as nuncio to the

---

[1] U. Moricca, *Gregorii Magni Dialogi* (Rome 1924).

[2] See ch. 36.

Imperial Court at Constantinople, where he remained for six years. Shortly after his return to Rome he became abbot of St. Andrew's, and five years later, when Pelagius II died, the clergy and people of Rome elected him Pope. During his very active pontificate he continued to foster Benedictine monasticism, most notably in sending St. Augustine and his monks as missionaries to England and in writing the *Life and Miracles of St. Benedict*. From the time it was first published (594) this 'biography of the greatest monk, written by the greatest Pope, himself also a monk'—as Thomas Hodgkin terms it[3]—enjoyed wide popularity and contributed greatly toward making St. Benedict one of the most venerated figures in Christendom for centuries. In fact, apart from the Rule, it is the only historical source we have for the life and character of the Patriarch of Western Monks.

It is clear from the general preface in Book One that St. Gregory's chief reason for writing the *Dialogues* was to honor the memory of the saints of Italy and to edify and instruct his fellow countrymen. He wanted them to realize that they were living in a land of saints and that great miracles were as numerous among

---

[3] *Italy and Her Invaders* IV (Oxford 1896) 411.

the Fathers of Italy as they had been among
the Fathers of the Desert and elsewhere.[4] The
book was also written to comfort and en-
courage the people of Italy during one of the
most disheartening periods of their history.[5]
The wars between the Emperor Justinian and
the barbarian Goths for the mastery of the
country had left much of it a wilderness. Men
and women had to live in constant dread of
the savage Lombard hordes that swept down
into Italy in 568 and were still slaying and
pillaging wherever they turned. Floods and
plagues and a long series of famines added to
the general gloom. Many even felt that the
final destruction of the world was at hand.
After reading in the first three books of *Dialogues* about the many striking miracles performed in their very midst, how could they
question God's unfailing protection of His
people? Then in Book Four St. Gregory en-
deavored to strengthen their faith in the un-
seen hereafter by proving that the soul does

---

[4] St. Gregory was evidently inspired to undertake this work by the tradition of monastic biography which had already yielded the famous Lives
of St. Paul the Hermit, St. Anthony the Great, St.
Pachomius and St. Martin of Tours.

[5] Moricca, *Dialogi* 3.38, 225-28.

not perish with the body and can look forward to eternal happiness.

Such then was the general purpose the Pope had in mind in publishing the *Life and Miracles of St. Benedict*. Even by modern standards he was well qualified to undertake this work. It appeared within fifty years of St. Benedict's death, and the author was not only very familiar with Subiaco and Monte Cassino, where the saint had spent most of his life, but had also been in personal contact with his disciples. 'I was unable to learn about all his miraculous deeds,' he explains in the preface. 'But the few that I am going to relate I know from the lips of four of his own disciples,' whom he goes on to name and describe. Some further details were obtained from Exhilaratus, a monk of St. Gregory's own Monastery of St. Andrew (ch. 18), from a 'distinguished Anthony' (ch. 26) and from St. Benedict's disciple Peregrinus (ch. 27). These men had all been close to the events they reported and were undoubtedly eyewitnesses to many of them.

St. Gregory's eminent position among the Fathers and Doctors of the Church is an added guarantee for the substantial accuracy of his narrative. Whether some of the miracles and prophecies it contains were exaggerated before they reached him or could have been explained as the result of merely natural causes, it is impossible to say. But there can be no doubt of the Pope's well-founded conviction that St. Benedict's miracles were numerous and striking enough to mark him out among his contemporaries as the great wonder-worker of Italy.[6]

As the general title of the four books indicates, St. Gregory has presented his account in the form of a dialogue, a literary device quite common among the pagan classical authors as well as among the Fathers of the Church.[7] The discussion takes place between the author and his deacon Peter, and, as in the case of many earlier 'Dialogues,' the leading speaker completely dominates the conversation. He did not employ this literary form, however, merely as a means of interrupting his narrative from time to time and of adding a note of informality. Peter's remarks and suggestions, his questions and doubts were designed to give Pope Gregory an opportunity to draw spiritual lessons for his readers from the saint's miracles and life. Though only

---

[6] J. Chapman, *St. Benedict and the Sixth Century* (London 1929) 1-13.

[7] E.g., Plato, Cicero, St. Augustine, Sulpicius Severus.

incidental to the story, these digressions have great doctrinal value and contain the practical moral reflections for which St. Gregory is so famous. His discourses on divine revelation (ch. 16) and on contemplative prayer (ch. 35) are two notable examples.

Very likely Peter was also meant to be a spokesman for the members of the papal household, giving expression to the interest and enthusiasm with which they had watched the Pope compiling his narrative. For as St. Gregory mentioned in a letter to Maximian, the bishop of Syracuse, it was in answer to their urgent requests that he had originally decided to write about the saints of Italy.[8]

In addition, Peter's words help to indicate the logical order the author has observed in presenting the miracles and prophecies. For in harmony with his general purpose of showing St. Benedict's holiness by recounting his miraculous deeds, Pope Gregory does not follow the chronological order of events except in broadly outlining the saint's life and spiritual development. In the preface he accompanies him from his home in Norcia to Rome, the scene of his studies. Then comes the saint's

---

[8] *Epistolae* 3.50 (ed. Ewald-Hartmann, MGH Epist. I 206).

flight from the city to Affile and shortly after to the wilderness at Subiaco, where he spent three years in solitude preparing for his future work by a life of prayer and fasting (ch. 1). His decisive victory over the tempter marked the dramatic climax in his conquest of self (ch. 2). It left him ready for closer union with God, a fuller share in His miraculous powers and an active part in destroying the influence of Satan over souls (chs. 3-4). As Peter observes (ch. 8), the miracles St. Benedict performed among his disciples at Subiaco reveal him as a man filled with the spirit of all the just—of Moses (ch. 5), Eliseus (ch. 6), St. Peter (ch. 7), Elias and David (ch. 8)—or rather, Gregory explains, as a man filled with the Spirit of Christ.

Now that the evil spirit could no longer hope to threaten St. Benedict's purity of soul, he started to assail him outwardly by molesting his disciples and inciting Florentius, an unworthy priest, to slander and attack him. To escape the priest's envy, St. Benedict withdrew to Monte Cassino (ch. 8). His first three miracles there show how complete his mastery was over the common enemy of mankind, who kept trying to undermine his work and in helpless rage resorted to abusive insults (chs. 9-11). Gregory next considers the numerous occasions on which the saint manifested the spirit of prophecy by foretelling future events and reading the human heart (chs. 12-22). Then at Peter's request he describes him in his everyday life, showing the miraculous power of his word, his generosity and sympathy with the afflicted, and his boundless trust in almighty God (chs. 23-30). After that he answers another of Peter's questions by citing one instance where St. Benedict performed a miracle at will (ch. 31) and another where he raised a boy to life through prayer (ch. 32). After using St. Scholastica's miracle to show that even the saints cannot always have their wishes fulfilled (ch. 33), he mentions her death and the vision St. Benedict had of her soul as it entered heaven (ch. 34). This leads him to consider the high point in the saint's spiritual development, the great vision in which he beheld the whole world gathered up in a single ray of light (ch. 35).

Peter urges him to continue, but Gregory, pleading his desire to take up the lives of other holy men, briefly discusses St. Benedict's Rule for Monks (ch. 36) and closes with an account of his death and his entrance into heaven (ch. 37). Then comes an epilogue recalling one of the miracles that was wrought after his death through his intercession (ch. 38).

There are also three short references to the saint in the third and fourth books of the *Dialogues*. Mention is made in Book Three of the advice he gave the hermit Martin, who had chained himself to a rock inside his narrow cave. St. Benedict sent word to him that the love of Christ should keep him chained there instead of the iron chain he was using, and the saintly hermit heeded his advice (ch. 16). In Book Four there is a brief description of the great vision (ch. 8), followed by another vision involving two of St. Benedict's disciples (ch. 9).

The present translation is based on the text given in Moricca's critical edition of the *Dialogues*. The Douay Version was used in citing the Old Testament. Except where the Confraternity Version is mentioned in the footnotes, the New Testament quotations have been taken from Monsignor Ronald Knox's translation, with the kind permission of His Eminence the Cardinal Archbishop :of Westminster, who holds the copyright, and of Sheed & Ward, the publisher.

The translators are indebted to the late Father Alexius Hoffmann, O.S.B., whose translation of the *Life and Miracles of St. Benedict* they consulted throughout.

SELECT BIBLIOGRAPHY

Texts:

U. Moricca, *Gregorii Magni Dialogi* (Rome 1924) 4-6, 71-134.

J.-P. Migne, *Patrologia Latina* 66 (Paris 1847) 125-204.

Translations:

E. Gardner (ed.), *The Dialogues of St. Gregory the Great*, trans. P. W. (London 1911).

A. Hoffmann, *The Life and Miracles of St. Benedict* (Collegeville Minn. 1925).

Secondary Sources:

O. Bardenhewer, *Geschichte der altkirchlichen Literatur* V (Freiburg im Breisgau 1932).

P. Batiffol, *St. Gregory the Great*, trans. J. L. Stoddard (New York 1929).

J. Chapman, *St. Benedict and the Sixth Century* (London 1929).

L. Doyle, *St. Benedict's Rule for Monasteries* (Collegeville Minn. 1948).

E. S. Duckett, *The Gateway to the Middle Ages* (New York 1938).

F. H. Dudden, *Gregory the Great, His Place in History and Thought* (2 vols. New York 1905).

J. McCann, *St. Benedict* (New York 1937).

I. Schuster, *Storia di san Benedetto e dei suoi tempi* (Milan 1946).

L. Tosti, *St. Benedict, an Historical Discourse on His Life*, trans. W. Woods (London 1896).

CONTENTS

LIFE AND MIRACLES OF ST. BENEDICT

Founder and Abbot of the Monastery
Which is Known as the Citadel of Campania[1]

GREGORY

Some years ago there lived a man who was revered for the holiness of his life. Blessed Benedict was his name, and he was blessed also with God's grace. During his boyhood he showed mature understanding, and a strength of character far beyond his years kept his heart detached from every pleasure. Even while still living in the world, free to enjoy all it had to offer, he saw how empty it was and turned from it without regret.

He was born in Norcia[2] of distinguished parents, who sent him to Rome for a liberal education. When he found many of the students there abandoning themselves to vice, he decided to withdraw from the world he had been preparing to enter; for he was afraid that if he acquired any of its learning he would be

---

[1] The Abbey of Monte Cassino. For the origin of this earlier name, cf. ch. 8 n.10.

[2] A little town about seventy miles northeast of Rome. The saint was born around 480.

drawn down with them to his eternal ruin. In his desire to please God alone, he turned his back on further studies, gave up home and inheritance and resolved to embrace the religious life. He took this step, fully aware of his ignorance; yet he was truly wise, uneducated though he may have been.

I was unable to learn about all his miraculous deeds. But the few that I am going to relate I know from the lips of four of his own disciples: Constantine, the holy man who succeeded him as abbot; Valentinian, for many years superior of the monastery at the Lateran;[3] Simplicius, Benedict's second successor; and Honoratus, who is still abbot of the monastery where the man of God first lived.[4]

(1) When Benedict abandoned his studies to go into solitude, he was accompanied only by his nurse, who loved him dearly. As they were passing through Affile, a number of devout men invited them to stay there and provided them with lodging near the Church of St. Peter.[1] One day, after asking her neigh-

---

[3] Next to the Lateran Basilica in Rome.

[4] Namely, Subiaco.

(1) [1] Literally 'in the Church of St. Peter'; most likely in a hospice attached to the church. Affile is about thirty-five miles east of Rome.

bors to lend her a tray for cleaning wheat, the nurse happened to leave it on the edge of the table and when she came back found it had slipped off and broken in two. The poor woman burst into tears; she had just borrowed this tray and now it was ruined. Benedict, who had always been a devout and thoughtful boy, felt sorry for his nurse when he saw her weeping. Quietly picking up both the pieces, he knelt down by himself and prayed earnestly to God, even to the point of tears. No sooner had he finished his prayer than he noticed that the two pieces were joined together again, without even a mark to show where the tray had been broken. Hurrying back at once, he cheerfully reassured his nurse and handed her the tray in perfect condition.

News of the miracle spread to all the country around Affile and stirred up so much admiration among the people that they hung the tray at the entrance of their church. Ever since then it has been a reminder to all of the great holiness Benedict had acquired at the very outset of his monastic life. The tray remained there many years for everyone to see, and it is still hanging over the doorway of the church in these days of Lombard power.[2] Benedict, however, preferred to suffer ill-treatment from the world rather than enjoy its praises. He wanted to spend himself laboring for God, not to be honored by the applause of men. So he stole away secretly from his nurse and fled to a lonely wilderness about thirty-five miles from Rome called Subiaco. A stream of cold, clear water running through the region broadens out at this point to form a lake, then flows off and continues on its course.[3] On his way there Benedict met a monk named Romanus, who asked him where he was going. After discovering the young man's purpose, Romanus kept it secret and even helped him carry it out by clothing him with the monastic habit and supplying his needs as well as he could.

At Subiaco, Benedict made his home in a narrow cave and for three years remained con-

---

[2] The Lombards, a Germanic people, left their homes along the upper Danube and invaded Italy in 568, establishing a kingdom there which lasted until 774.

[3] Subiaco lies along the Anio River about five miles north of Affile. The lake St. Gregory speaks of gave the site its Latin name of *Sublacum*. It was formed by a dam which the Emperor Claudius had built across the river, and lasted until 1305 when the dam was destroyed by floods.

cealed there unknown to anyone except the monk Romanus, who lived in a monastery close by under the rule of Abbot Deodatus. With fatherly concern this monk regularly set aside as much bread as he could from his own portion; then from time to time, unnoticed by his abbot, he left the monastery long enough to take the bread to Benedict. There was no path leading from the monastery down to his cave on account of a cliff that rose directly over it. To reach him Romanus had to tie the bread to the end of a long rope and lower it over the cliff. A little bell attached to the rope let Benedict know when the bread was there, and he would come out to get it. The ancient enemy of mankind grew envious of the kindness shown by the older monk in supplying Benedict with food, and one day, as the bread was being lowered, he threw a stone at the bell and broke it. Yet in spite of this, Romanus kept on with his faithful service.

At length the time came when almighty God wished to grant him rest from his toil and reveal Benedict's virtuous life to others. Like a shining lamp his example was to be set on a lampstand to give light to everyone in God's house.[4] The Lord therefore appeared in

---

[4] Cf. Matt. 5.15.

a vision to a priest some distance away who had just prepared his Easter dinner. 'How can you prepare these delicacies for yourself,' He asked, 'while my servant is out there in the wilds suffering from hunger?'

Rising at once, the priest wrapped up the food and set out to find the man of God even though it was Easter Sunday. He searched for him along the rough mountainsides, in the valleys and through the caverns, until he found him hidden in the cave. They said a prayer of thanksgiving together and then sat down to talk about the spiritual life. After a while the priest suggested that they take their meal. 'Today is the great feast of Easter,' he added.

'It must be a great feast to have brought me this kind visit,' the man of God replied, not realizing after his long separation from men that that day was Easter Sunday.

'Today is really Easter,' the priest insisted, 'the feast of our Lord's Resurrection. On such a solemn occasion you should not be fasting. Besides, I was sent here by almighty God so that both of us could share in His gifts.'

After that they said grace and began their meal. When it was over they conversed some more, and then the priest went back to his church.[5]

---

[5] Cf. Acts 9.10-19.

At about the same time some shepherds also discovered Benedict's hiding place. When they first looked through the thickets and caught sight of him clothed in rough skins, they mistook him for some wild animal. Soon, however, they recognized in him a servant of God, and many of them gave up their sinful ways for a life of holiness. As a result his name became known to all the people in that locality and great numbers visited his cave, supplying him with the food he needed and receiving from his lips in return spiritual food for their souls.

(2) One day while the saint was alone, the tempter came in the form of a little blackbird, which began to flutter in front of his face. It kept so close that he could easily have caught it in his hand. Instead he made the sign of the Cross and the bird flew away. The moment it left, he was seized with an unusually violent temptation. The evil spirit recalled to his mind a woman he had once seen, and before he realized it his emotions were carrying him away. Almost overcome in the struggle, he was on the point of abandoning the lonely wilderness, when suddenly with the help of God's grace he came to himself.

Just then he noticed a thick patch of nettles and briers next to him. Throwing his garment aside, he flung himself naked into the sharp thorns and stinging nettles. There he rolled and tossed until his whole body was in pain and covered with blood. Yet once he had conquered pleasure through suffering, his torn and bleeding skin served to drain off the poison of temptation from his body. Before long the pain that was burning his whole body had put out the fires of evil in his heart. It was by exchanging these two fires that he gained the victory over sin. So complete was his triumph that from then on, as he later told his disciples, he never experienced another temptation of this kind.

Soon after, many forsook the world to place themselves under his guidance, for now that he was free from these temptations he was ready to instruct others in the practice of virtue. That is why Moses commanded the Levites to begin their service when they were twenty-five years old and to become guardians of the sacred vessels only at the age of fifty.[1]

PETER

The meaning of the passage you quote is becoming a little clearer to me now. Still I wish you would explain it more fully.

---

(2)   [1] Cf. Num. 8.24-26.

GREGORY

It is a well-known fact, Peter, that temptations of the flesh are violent during youth, whereas after the age of fifty concupiscence dies down. Now, the sacred vessels are the souls of the faithful. God's chosen servants must therefore obey and serve and tire themselves out with strenuous work as long as they are still subject to temptations. Only when full maturity has left them undisturbed by evil thoughts are they put in charge of the sacred vessels, for then they become teachers of souls.

PETER

I like the way you interpreted that passage. Now that you have explained what it means, I hope you will continue with your account of the holy man's life.

GREGORY

(3) With the passing of this temptation Benedict's soul, like a field cleared of briers, soon yielded a rich harvest of virtues. As word spread of his saintly life, the renown of his name increased. One day the entire community from a nearby monastery[1] came to see him. Their abbot had recently died, and they

---

(3) [1] Usually identified as Vicovaro, about twenty miles lower down the Anio.

wanted the man of God to be their new superior. For some time he tried to discourage them by refusing their request, warning them that his way of life would never harmonize with theirs. But they kept insisting until in the end he gave his consent.

At the monastery he watched carefully over the religious spirit of his monks and would not tolerate any of their previous disobedience. No one was allowed to turn from the straight path of monastic discipline either to the right or to the left. Their waywardness, however, clashed with the standards he upheld, and in their resentment they started to reproach themselves for choosing him as abbot. It only made them the more sullen to find him curbing every fault and evil habit. They could not see why they should have to force their settled minds into new ways of thinking.

At length, proving once again that the very life of the just is a burden to the wicked,[2] they tried to find a means of doing away with him and decided to poison his wine. A glass pitcher containing this poisoned drink was presented to the man of God during his meal for the customary blessing. As he made the sign

---

[2] Cf. Wisd. 2.12-20.

of the Cross over it with his hand, the pitcher was shattered even though it was well beyond his reach at the time. It broke at his blessing as if he had struck it with a stone.

Then he realized it had contained a deadly drink which could not bear the sign of life. Still calm and undisturbed, he rose at once and after gathering the community together addressed them. 'May almighty God have mercy on you,' he said. 'Why did you conspire to do this? Did I not tell you at the outset that my way of life would never harmonize with yours? Go and find yourselves an abbot to your liking. It is impossible for me to stay here any longer.' Then he went back to the wilderness he loved, to live alone with himself in the presence of his heavenly Father.

PETER

I am not quite sure I understand what you mean by saying 'to live with himself.'

GREGORY

These monks had an outlook on religious life entirely unlike his own and were all conspiring against him. Now, if he had tried to force them to remain under his rule, he might have forfeited his own fervor and peace of soul and even turned his eyes from the light of contemplation. Their persistent daily faults would have left him almost too weary to correct his own, and he would have been in danger of losing sight of himself without finding them. You see, Peter, great anxieties can carry us out of ourselves almost entirely. Every time this happens, we are no longer with ourselves even though we still remain what we are; we are too busy with other matters to look into our own souls.

Surely we cannot describe as 'with himself' the young man who traveled to a distant country where he wasted his inheritance and then, after hiring himself out to one of its citizens to feed swine, had to watch them eat their fill of pods while he went hungry. Do we not read in Scripture that as he was considering all he had lost 'he came to himself and said, "How many hired servants there are in my father's house who have more bread than they can eat" '?[3] If he was already 'with himself,' how could he have come 'to himself'?

Blessed Benedict, on the contrary, can be said to have lived 'with himself' because at all times he kept such close watch over his life and actions. By searching continually into his own soul he always beheld himself in the presence of his Creator. And this kept his mind from straying off to the world outside.

---

[3] Luke 15.17.

PETER

But what of Peter the apostle when he was led out of prison by an angel? According to the Scriptures, he too 'came to himself and said, "Now I know for certain that the Lord has sent his angel and rescued me from the power of Herod and from all that the Jewish people were expecting." '[4]

GREGORY

There are two ways in which we can be carried out of ourselves, Peter. Either we fall below ourselves through sins of thought, or we are lifted above ourselves by the grace of contemplation. The young man who fed the swine sank below himself as a result of his shiftless ways and his unclean life. The apostle Peter was also out of himself when the angel set him free and raised him to a state of ecstasy, but he was above himself. In coming to themselves again, the former had to break with his sinful past before he could find his true and better self, whereas the latter merely returned from the heights of contemplation to his ordinary state of mind.

Now the saintly Benedict really lived 'with himself' out in that lonely wilderness by always keeping his thoughts recollected. Yet

---

[4] Acts 12.11 (Confraternity Version).

he must have left his own self far below each
time he was drawn heavenward in fervent
contemplation.

PETER

I am very grateful to you for that explanation. Do you think it was right, though, for
him to forsake this community, once he had
taken it under his care?

GREGORY

In my opinion, Peter, a superior ought to
bear patiently with a community of evil men
as long as it has some devout members who
can benefit from his presence. When none of
the members are devout enough to give any
promise of good results, his efforts to help
such a community will prove to be a serious
mistake, especially if there are opportunities
nearby to work more fruitfully for God. Was
there anyone the holy man could have hoped
to protect by staying where he was, after he
saw that they were all united against him?

In this matter we cannot afford to overlook
the attitude of the saints. When they find
their work producing no results in one place,
they move on to another where it will do some
good. This explains the action of the blessed
apostle Paul. In order to escape from Damascus, where he was being persecuted, he se-
cured a basket and a rope and had himself

secretly lowered over the wall.[5] Yet this outstanding preacher of the Gospel longed to depart and be with Christ, since for him life meant Christ, and death was a prize to be won.[6] Besides being eager for the trials of persecution himself, he even inspired others to endure them.[7] Can we say that Paul feared death, when he expressly declared that he longed to die for the love of Christ? Surely not. But when he saw how little he was accomplishing at Damascus in spite of all his toil, he saved himself for more fruitful labors elsewhere. God's fearless warrior refused to be held back inside the walls and sought the open field of battle.

And if you do not mind continuing to listen, Peter, you will soon discover that after blessed Benedict left that obstinate community he restored to life many another soul that was spiritually dead.

PETER

I am sure your conclusion is correct, after the simple proof you gave and that striking example from Sacred Scripture. Would you be good enough to return now to the story of this great abbot's life?

---

[5] Cf. Acts 9.25; 2 Cor. 11.32-33.
[6] Cf. Phil. 1.21,23.
[7] Cf. Heb. 10.32-36.

GREGORY

As Benedict's influence spread over the surrounding countryside because of his signs and
wonders, a great number of men gathered
around him to devote themselves to God's service. Christ blessed his work and before long
he had established twelve monasteries there,
with an abbot and twelve monks in each of
them. There were a few other monks whom
he kept with him, since he felt that they still
needed his personal guidance.

It was about this time that pious noblemen
from Rome first came to visit the saint and
left their sons with him to be schooled in the
service of God. Thus Euthicius[8] brought his
son Maurus, and the senator Tertullus,
Placid, both very promising boys. Maurus, in
fact, who was a little older, had already acquired solid virtue and was soon very help-
ful to his saintly master. But Placid was still
only a child.

(4)   In one of the monasteries Benedict had
founded in that locality, there was a monk
who would never remain with the rest of the
community for silent prayer. Instead he left
the chapel as soon as they knelt down to

---

[8] Usually written 'Equitius,' but 'Euthicius' is
the critical reading.

pray, and passed the time aimlessly at whatever happened to interest him. His abbot cor-
rected him repeatedly and then at length sent
him to the man of God. This time the monk
received a stern rebuke for his folly and after
his return took the correction to heart for a
day or two, only to fall back the third day
into his old habit of wandering off during the
time of prayer. On learning of this from the
abbot, the man of God sent word that he was
coming over himself to see that the monk
mended his ways.

Upon his arrival at the monastery Benedict
joined the community in the chapel at the
regular hour. After they had finished chanting
the Psalms and had begun their silent prayer,
he noticed that the restless monk was drawn
outside by a little black boy who was pulling
at the edge of his habit.

'Do you see who is leading that monk out
of the chapel?' he whispered to Abbot Pompeianus and Maurus.

'No,' they replied.

'Let us pray then,' he said, 'that you may
see what is happening to him.'

They prayed for two days, and after that
Maurus also saw what was taking place, but
Abbot Pompeianus still could not. The next

day when prayers were over, Benedict found the offender loitering outside and struck him with his staff for being so obstinate of heart. From then on the monk remained quietly at prayer like the rest, without being bothered again by the tempter. It was as if that ancient enemy had been struck by the blow himself and was afraid to domineer over the monk's thoughts any longer.

(5) Three of the monasteries the saint had built close by stood on the bare rocky heights. It was a real hardship for these monks always to go down to the lake to get water for their daily needs. Besides, the slope was steep and they found the descent very dangerous. The members of the three communities therefore came in a body to see the servant of God. After explaining how difficult it was for them to climb down the mountainside every day for their water supply, they assured him that the only solution was to have the monasteries moved somewhere else.

Benedict answered them with fatherly words of encouragement and sent them back. That same night, in company with the little boy Placid, he climbed to the rocky heights and prayed there for a long time. On finishing his prayer he placed three stones together to indicate the spot where he had knelt and then went back to his monastery unnoticed by anyone.

The following day, when the monks came again with their request, he told them to go to the summit of the mountain. 'You will find three stones there,' he said, 'one on top of the other. If you dig down a little, you will see that almighty God has the power to bring forth water even from that rocky summit and in His goodness relieve you of the hardship of such a long climb.'

Going back to the place he had described, they noticed that the surface was already moist. As soon as they had dug the ground away, water filled the hollow and welled up in such abundance that today a full stream is still flowing down from the top of the mountain into the ravine below.[1]

(6) At another time a simple, sincere Goth came to Subiaco to become a monk, and blessed Benedict was very happy to admit him. One day he had him take a brush hook and clear away the briers from a place at the edge of the lake where a garden was to be planted. While the Goth was hard at work cutting down the thick brush, the iron blade slipped off the handle and flew into a very deep part

---

(5) [1] Cf. Exod. 17.1-7; Num. 20.1-11.

of the lake, where there was no hope of re-covering it.

At this the poor man ran trembling to Maurus and after describing the accident told him how sorry he was for his carelessness. Maurus in turn informed the servant of God, who on hearing what had happened went down to the lake, took the handle from the Goth and thrust it in the water. Immediately the iron blade rose from the bottom of the lake and slipped back onto the handle.[1] Then he handed the tool back to the Goth and told him, 'Continue with your work now. There is no need to be upset.'

(7) Once while blessed Benedict was in his room, one of his monks, the boy Placid, went down to get some water. In letting the bucket fill too rapidly, he lost his balance and was pulled into the lake, where the current quickly seized him and carried him about a stone's throw from the shore. Though inside the monastery at the time, the man of God was instantly aware of what had happened and called out to Maurus: 'Hurry, Brother Maurus! The boy who just went down for water has fallen into the lake, and the current is carry-ing him away.'

---

(6)   [1] Cf. 4 Kings 6.4-7.

What followed was remarkable indeed, and unheard of since the time of Peter the apostle![1] Maurus asked for the blessing and on receiving it hurried out to fulfill his abbot's command. He kept on running even over the water till he reached the place where Placid was drifting along helplessly. Pulling him up by the hair, Maurus rushed back to shore, still under the impression that he was on dry land. It was only when he set foot on the ground that he came to himself and looking back realized that he had been running on the surface of the water. Overcome with fear and amazement at a deed he would never have thought possible, he returned to his abbot and told him what had taken place.

The holy man would not take any personal credit for the deed but attributed it to the obedience of his disciple. Maurus on the contrary claimed that it was due entirely to his abbot's command. He could not have been responsible for the miracle himself, he said, since he had not even known he was performing it. While they were carrying on this friendly contest of humility, the question was settled by the boy who had been rescued. 'When I was being drawn out of the water,'

---

(7)   [1] Cf. Matt. 14.28-29.

he told them, 'I saw the abbot's cloak over my head; he is the one I thought was bringing me to shore.'

PETER

What marvelous deeds these are! They are sure to prove inspiring to all who hear of them. Indeed, the more you tell me about this great man, the more eager I am to keep on listening.

GREGORY

(8) By this time the people of that whole region for miles around had grown fervent in their love for Christ, and many of them had forsaken the world in order to bring their hearts under the light yoke of the Savior. Now, in a neighboring church there was a priest named Florentius, the grandfather of our subdeacon Florentius. Urged on by the bitter enemy of mankind, this priest set out to undermine the saint's work. And, envious as the wicked always are of the holiness in others which they are not striving to acquire themselves, he denounced Benedict's way of life and kept everyone he could from visiting him.

The progress of the saint's work, however, could not be stopped. His reputation for holiness kept on growing and with it the number of vocations to a more perfect state of life.

This only infuriated Florentius all the more. He still longed to enjoy the praise the saint was receiving, yet he was unwilling to lead a praiseworthy life himself. At length his soul became so blind with jealousy that he decided to poison a loaf of bread and send it to the servant of God as a sign of Christian fellowship. Though aware at once of the deadly poison it contained, Benedict thanked him for the gift.

At mealtime a raven used to come out of the nearby woods to receive food from the saint's hands. On this occasion he set the poisoned loaf in front of it and said, 'In the name of our Lord Jesus Christ, take this bread and carry it to a place where no one will be able to find it.' The raven started to caw and circled around the loaf of bread with open beak and flapping wings as if to indicate that it was willing to obey but found it impossible to do so. Several times the saint repeated the command. 'Take the bread,' he said, 'and do not be afraid! Take it away from here and leave it where no one can find it.' After hesitating for a long while the raven finally took the loaf in its beak and flew away. About three hours later, when it had disposed of the bread, it returned and received its usual meal from the hands of the man of God.

The saintly abbot now realized how deep the resentment of his enemy was, and he felt grieved not so much for his own sake as for the priest's. But Florentius, after his failure to do away with the master, determined instead to destroy the souls of the disciples and for this purpose sent seven depraved women into the garden of Benedict's monastery. There they joined hands and danced together for some time within sight of his followers, in an attempt to lead them into sin.

When the saint noticed this from his window, he began to fear that some of his younger monks might go astray. Convinced that the priest's hatred for him was the real cause of this attack, he let envy have its way and taking only a few monks with him set out to find a new home. Before he left he reorganized all the monasteries he had founded, appointing priors to assist in governing them, and adding some new members to the communities.

Hardly had the man of God made his humble escape from all this bitterness when almighty God struck the priest down with terrible vengeance. As he was standing on the balcony of his house congratulating himself on Benedict's departure, the structure suddenly collapsed, crushing him to death; yet the rest of the building remained undamaged. This accident occurred before the saint was even ten miles away. His disciple Maurus immediately decided to send a messenger with the news and ask him to return, now that the priest who had caused him so much trouble was dead. Benedict was overcome with sorrow and regret on hearing this, for not only had his enemy been killed, but one of his own disciples had rejoiced over his death. And for showing pleasure in sending such a message he gave Maurus a penance to perform.

PETER

This whole account is really amazing. The water streaming from the rock reminds me of Moses,[1] and the iron blade that rose from the bottom of the lake, of Eliseus.[2] The walking on the water recalls St. Peter;[3] the obedience of the raven, Elias;[4] and the grief at the death of an enemy, David.[5] This man must have been filled with the spirit of all the just.

GREGORY

Actually, Peter, blessed Benedict possessed

---

(8) [1] Cf. Exod. 17.1-7; Num. 20.1-11.
     [2] Cf. 4 Kings 6.4-7.
     [3] Cf. Matt. 14.28-29.
     [4] Cf. 3 Kings 17.6.
     [5] Cf. 2 Kings 1.11-12; 18.33.

the Spirit of only one Person, the Savior who fills the hearts of all the faithful by granting them the fruits of His Redemption. For St. John says of Him, 'There is one who enlightens every soul born into the world; he was the true light.'[6] And again, 'Of his fullness we have all received.'[7] Holy men were never able to hand on to others the miraculous powers which they received from God. Our Savior was the only one to give His followers the power to work signs and wonders, just as He alone could assure His enemies that He would give them the sign of the prophet Jonas.[8] Seeing this sign fulfilled in His death, the proud looked on with scorn. The humble, who saw its complete fulfillment in His rising from the dead, turned to Him with reverence and love. In this mystery, then, the proud beheld Him dying in disgrace, while the humble witnessed His triumph over death.

PETER

Now that you have finished explaining this, please tell me where the holy man settled after his departure. Do you know whether he performed any more miracles?

---

[6] John 1.9.
[7] *Ibid*. 1.16 (Confraternity Version).
    Cf. Matt. 12.39-40.

GREGORY

Although he moved to a different place,
Peter, his enemy remained the same. In fact,
the assaults he had to endure after this were
all the more violent, because the very master
of evil was fighting against him in open
battle.

The fortified town of Cassino lies at the
foot of a towering mountain that shelters it
within its slope and stretches upward over a
distance of nearly three miles.[9] On its summit
stood a very old temple, in which the igno-
rant country people still worshiped Apollo
as their pagan ancestors had done, and went
on offering superstitious and idolatrous sac-
rifices in groves dedicated to various demons.

When the man of God arrived at this spot,
he destroyed the idol, overturned the altar
and cut down the trees in the sacred groves.[10]

---

[9] St. Gregory must be referring to the winding
path that led up the mountain. The altitude of
Monte Cassino is 1700 feet.

[10] Monte Cassino is about seventy-five miles
southeast of Rome. St. Benedict arrived there in
529. In addition to the pagan shrines mentioned by
St. Gregory, there was also a very ancient fortress
on the summit for the defense of the townspeople
below and the surrounding plains. The Abbey of
Monte Cassino was built entirely within the walls
of the fortress and was for that reason known at

Then he turned the temple of Apollo into a chapel dedicated to St. Martin,[11] and where Apollo's altar had stood, he built a chapel in honor of St. John the Baptist. Gradually the people of the countryside were won over to the true faith by his zealous preaching.

Such losses the ancient enemy could not bear in silence. This time he did not appear to the saint in a dream or under a disguise but met him face to face and objected fiercely to the outrages he had to endure. His shouts were so loud that the brethren heard him too, although they were unable to see him. According to the saint's own description, the devil had an appearance utterly revolting to human eyes. He was enveloped in fire, and when he raged against the man of God, flames darted from his eyes and mouth. Everyone could hear what he was saying. First he called Benedict by name. Then, finding that the saint would not answer, he broke out in abusive language. 'Benedict, Benedict, blessed

---

first as the Citadel of Campania, as we learn from the full title of this book. Cf. L. Tosti, *St. Benedict, an Historical Discourse on His Life*, trans. W. Woods (London 1896) 83-86; Cardinal Schuster, *Storia di san Benedetto e dei suoi tempi* (Milan 1946) 127, 129, 150.

[11] St. Martin of Tours.

Benedict!' he would begin, and then add, 'You cursed Benedict! Cursed, not blessed! What do you want with me? Why are you tormenting me like this?'

From now on, Peter, as you can well imagine, the devil fought against the man of God with renewed violence. But contrary to his plans, all these attacks only supplied the saint with further opportunities for victory.

(9) One day while the monks were constructing a section of the abbey, they noticed a rock lying close at hand and decided to use it in the building. When two or three did not succeed in lifting it, others joined in to help. Yet it remained fixed in its place as though it was rooted to the ground. Then they were sure that the devil himself was sitting on this stone and preventing them from moving it in spite of all their efforts.

Faced with this difficulty, they asked Abbot Benedict to come and use his prayers to drive away the devil who was holding down the rock. The saint began to pray as soon as he got there, and after he had finished and made the sign of the Cross, the monks picked up the rock with such ease that it seemed to have lost all its previous weight.

(10) The abbot then directed them to spade up the earth where the stone had been.

When they had dug a little way into the ground they came upon a bronze idol, which they threw into the kitchen for the time being. Suddenly the kitchen appeared to be on fire and everyone felt that the entire building was going up in flames. The noise and commotion they made in their attempt to put out the blaze by pouring on buckets of water brought Benedict to the scene. Unable to see the fire which appeared so real to his monks, he quietly bowed his head in prayer and soon had opened their eyes to the foolish mistake they were making. Now, instead of the flames the evil spirit had devised, they once more saw the kitchen standing intact

(11) On another occasion they were working on one of the walls that had to be built a little higher. The man of God was in his room at the time praying, when the devil appeared to him and remarked sarcastically that he was on his way to visit the brethren at their work. Benedict quickly sent them word to be on their guard against the evil spirit who would soon be with them. Just as they received his warning, the devil overturned the wall, crushing under its ruins the body of a very young monk who was the son of a tax collector.

Unconcerned about the damaged wall in their grief and dismay over the loss of their

brother, the monks hurried to Abbot Benedict to let him know of the dreadful accident.
He told them to bring the mangled body to his
room. It had to be carried in on a blanket, for
the wall had not only broken the boy's arms
and legs but had crushed all the bones in his
body. The saint had the remains placed on
the reed matting where he used to pray and
after that told them all to leave. Then he
closed the door and knelt down to offer his
most earnest prayers to God. That very hour,
to the astonishment of all, he sent the boy
back to his work as sound and healthy as he
had been before.[1] Thus, in spite of the devil's
attempt to mock the man of God by causing
this tragic death, the young monk was able to
rejoin his brethren and help them finish the
wall.

Meanwhile Benedict began to manifest the
spirit of prophecy by foretelling future events
and by describing to those who were with him
what they had done in his absence.

(12) It was a custom of the house, strictly
observed as a matter of regular discipline, that
monks away on business did not take food or
drink outside the monastery.[1] One day a few

---

(11)   [1] Cf. Acts 9.40-41.
(12)   [1] Cf. L. Doyle, *St. Benedict's Rule for Monasteries*
        (Collegeville Minn. 1948) 51.66.

of them went out on an assignment which kept them occupied till rather late. They stopped for a meal at the house of a devout woman they knew in the neighborhood. On their return, when they presented themselves to the abbot for the usual blessing, he asked them where they had taken their meal.

'Nowhere,' they answered.

'Why are you lying to me?' he said. 'Did you not enter the house of this particular woman and eat these various foods and have so and so many cups to drink?'

On hearing him mention the woman's hospitality and exactly what she had given them to eat and drink, they clearly recalled the wrong they had done, fell trembling at his feet and confessed their guilt. The man of God did not hesitate to pardon them, confident that they would do no further wrong in his absence, since they now realized he was always present with them in spirit.

(13) The monk Valentinian, mentioned earlier in our narrative, had a brother who was a very devout layman. Every year he visited the abbey in order to get Benedict's blessing and see his brother. On the way he always used to fast. Now, one time as he was making this journey he was joined by another traveler who had brought some food along.

'Come,' said the stranger after some time had passed, 'let us have something to eat before we become too fatigued.'

'I am sorry,' the devout layman replied. 'I always fast on my way to visit Abbot Benedict.'

After that the traveler was quiet for a while. But when they had walked along some distance together, he repeated his suggestion. Still mindful of his good resolve, Valentinian's brother again refused. His companion did not insist and once more agreed to accompany him a little furthur without eating.

Then, after they had covered a great distance together and were very tired from the long hours of walking, they came upon a meadow and a spring. The whole setting seemed ideal for a much needed rest. 'Look,' said the stranger, 'water and a meadow! What a delightful spot for us to have some refreshments! A little rest will give us strength to finish our journey without any discomfort.'

It was such an attractive sight and this third invitation sounded so appealing that the devout layman was completely won over and stopped there to eat with his companion. Toward evening he arrived at the monastery and was presented to the abbot. As soon as he asked for the blessing, however, the holy

man reproved him for his conduct on the journey. 'How is it,' he said, 'that the evil spirit
who spoke with you in the person of your
traveling companion could not persuade you
to do his will the first and second time he
tried, but succeeded in his third attempt?' At
this Valentinian's brother fell at Benedict's
feet and admitted the weakness of his will.
The thought that even from such a distance
the saint had witnessed the wrong he had
done filled him with shame and remorse.

PETER

This proves that the servant of God possessed the spirit of Eliseus. He, too, was present
with one of his followers who was far away.[1]

GREGORY

If you will listen a little longer, Peter, I
have an incident to tell you that is even more
astonishing. (14) Once while the Goths
were still in power Totila their king happened
to be marching in the direction of Benedict's
monastery.[1] When still some distance away he

---

(13)   [1] Cf. 4 Kings 5.25-27.

(14)   [1] The Ostrogoths were a Germanic people from
          Eastern Europe who had established their king-
          dom in Italy under Theodoric in 493. King Totila
          (541-52) was fighting to re-establish Gothic pow-
          er there after it had virtually been broken by the
          Emperor Justinian's armies during the previous

halted with his troops and sent a messenger
ahead to announce his coming, for he had
heard that the man of God possessed the gift
of prophecy. As soon as he received word that
he would be welcome, the crafty king decided
to put the saint's prophetic powers to a test.
He had Riggo, his sword-bearer, fitted out
with royal robes and riding boots and directed
him to go in this disguise to the man of God.
Vul, Ruderic and Blidin, three men from his
own bodyguard, were to march at his side as
if he really were the king of the Goths. To
supplement these marks of kingship, Totila
also provided him with a sword-bearer and
other attendants.

As Riggo entered the monastery grounds in
his kingly robes and with all his attendants,
Benedict caught sight of him and as soon as
the company came within hearing called out
from where he sat. 'Son, lay aside the robes
that you are wearing,' he said. 'Lay them
aside. They do not belong to you.' Aghast at
seeing what a great man he had tried to mock,
Riggo sank to the ground, and with him all
the members of his company. Even after they
had risen to their feet they did not dare ap-

decade. The following events probably took place
when Totila was marching on Naples, which he
captured in 543.

proach the saint but hurried back in alarm to tell their king how quickly they had been detected.

(15)   King Totila then went to the monastery in person. The moment he noticed the man of God sitting at a distance, he was afraid to come any closer and fell down prostrate where he was. Two or three times Benedict asked him to rise. When Totila still hesitated to do so in his presence, the servant of Christ walked over to him and with his own hands helped him from the ground. Then he rebuked the king for his crimes and briefly foretold everything that was going to happen to him. 'You are the cause of many evils,' he said. 'You have caused many in the past. Put an end now to your wickedness. You will enter Rome and cross the sea. You have nine more years to rule, and in the tenth year you will die.'

Terrified at these words, the king asked for a blessing and went away. From that time on he was less cruel. Not long after, he went to Rome and then crossed over to Sicily. In the tenth year of his reign he lost his kingdom and his life as almighty God had decreed.

There is also a story about the bishop of

Canosa,[1] who made regular visits to the abbey and stood high in Benedict's esteem because of his saintly life. Once while they were discussing Totila's invasion and the downfall of Rome, the bishop said, 'The city will be destroyed by this king and left without a single inhabitant.'

'No,' Benedict assured him, 'Rome will not be destroyed by the barbarians. It will be shaken by tempests and lightnings, hurricanes and earthquakes, until finally it lies buried in its own ruins.'[2]

The meaning of this prophecy is perfectly clear to us now. We have watched the walls of Rome crumble and have seen its homes in ruins, its churches destroyed by violent storms, and its dilapidated buildings surrounded by their own debris.

Benedict's disciple Honoratus, who told me about the prophecy, admits he did not hear it personally, but he assures me that some of his own brethren gave him this account of it.

---

(15) [1] In southeastern Italy, about 120 miles from
        Monte Cassino.
        [2] This conversation is the chief reason why 547
        has now been generally accepted as the year of St.
        Benedict's death. The two were evidently discussing the siege Totila began in October 545,
        which ended with his capture of the city in De-

(16) At about the same time there was a cleric from the church of Aquino[1] who was being tormented by an evil spirit. Constantius, his saintly bishop, had already sent him to the shrines of various martyrs in the hope that he would be cured. But the holy martyrs did not grant him this favor, preferring instead to reveal the wonderful gifts of the servant of God.

As soon as the cleric was brought to him, Benedict drove out the evil spirit with fervent prayers to Christ.[2] Before sending him back to Aquino, however, he told him to abstain from meat thereafter and never to ad-

---

cember 546. Cf. J. McCann, *St. Benedict* (New York 1937) 208-10. The fulfillment of the first part of St. Benedict's prophecy appears almost miraculous, for on this occasion the king was determined to level the entire city to the ground. He had already demolished a third of its walled defenses and was ready to set fire to all its buildings, when a plea from the shrewd imperial general Belisarius to spare 'the greatest and most glorious of all the cities under the sun, . . . the most wonderful sight in the world,' persuaded him to stop. Cf. T. Hodgkin, *Italy and Her Invaders* IV (Oxford 1896) 500-02.

(16) [1] About five miles from Monte Cassino.
[2] Cf. Mark 16.17.

vance to sacred orders.[3] 'If you ignore this
warning,' he added, 'and present yourself for
ordination, you will find yourself once more
in the power of Satan.'

The cleric left completely cured, and as
long as his previous torments were still fresh
in his mind he did exactly as the man of God
had ordered. Then, with the passing of years,
all his seniors in the clerical state died, and he
had to watch newly ordained young men
moving ahead of him in rank. Finally he pre-
tended to have forgotten about the saint's
warning and, disregarding it, presented himself for ordination. Instantly he was seized by
the devil and tormented mercilessly until he
died.

PETER

The servant of God must even have been
aware of the hidden designs of Providence, to
have realized that this cleric had been handed
over to Satan[4] to keep him from aspiring to
holy orders.

---

[3] Only the priesthood and the diaconate were
regarded as sacred or holy orders before the twelfth
century, when the subdiaconate also came to be
included among them. Cf. P. de Puniet, *The Roman
Pontifical, a History and Commentary*, trans. M. Har-
court (London 1932) 150.

[4] Cf. 1 Cor. 5.5.

GREGORY

Is there any reason why a person who has observed the commandments of God should not also know of God's secret designs? 'The man who unites himself to the Lord becomes one spirit with him,'[5] we read in Sacred Scripture.

PETER

If everyone who unites himself to the Lord becomes one spirit with him, what does the renowned Apostle mean when he asks, 'Who has ever understood the Lord's thoughts, or been his counselor?'[6] It hardly seems possible to be one spirit with a person without knowing his thoughts.

GREGORY

Holy men do know the Lord's thoughts, Peter, in so far as they are one with Him. This is clear from the Apostle's words, 'Who else can know a man's thoughts, except the man's own spirit that is within him? So no one else can know God's thoughts but the Spirit of God.'[7] To show that he actually knew God's thoughts, St. Paul added: 'And what we have received is no spirit of worldly wisdom; it is

---

[5] 1 Cor. 6.17
[6] Rom. 11.34.
[7] 1 Cor. 2.11.

the Spirit that comes from God.'[8] And again:
'No eye has seen, no ear has heard, no human
heart conceived, the welcome God has pre-
pared for those who love him. To us, then,
God has made a revelation of it through his
Spirit.'[9]

PETER

If it is true that God's thoughts were revealed to the Apostle by the Holy Spirit,
how could he introduce his statement with the
words, 'How deep is the mine of God's wisdom, of his knowledge; how inscrutable are
his judgments, how undiscoverable his ways!'[10]
Another difficulty just occurred to me now as
I was speaking. In addressing the Lord, David
the prophet declares, 'With my lips I have
pronounced all the judgments of thy mouth.'[11]
Surely it is a greater achievement to express
one's knowledge than merely to possess it.
How is it, then, that St. Paul calls the judgments of God inscrutable, whereas David says
he knows them all and has even pronounced
them with his lips?

---

[8] *Ibid*. 2.12.
[9] *Ibid*. 2.9.
[10] Rom. 11.33.
[11] Ps. 118.13.

GREGORY

I already gave a brief reply to both of these objections when I told you that holy men know God's thoughts in so far as they are one with Him.   For all who follow the Lord wholeheartedly are living in spiritual union with Him. As long as they are still weighed down with a perishable body, however, they are not actually united to Him. It is only to the extent that they are one with God that they know His hidden judgments. In so far as they are not yet one with Him, they do not know them. Since even holy men cannot fully grasp the secret designs of God during this present life, they call His judgments inscrutable. At the same time, they understand His judgments and can even pronounce them with their lips; for they keep their hearts united to God by dwelling continually on the words of Holy Scripture and on such private revelations as they may receive, until they grasp His meaning.   In other words, they do not know the judgments which God conceals but only those which He reveals. That is why, after declaring, 'With my lips I have pronounced all the judgments,' the prophet immediately adds the phrase, 'of thy mouth,'[12]

---

[12] *Ibid.*

as if to say, 'I can know and pronounce only the judgments You have spoken to me. Those You leave unspoken must remain hidden from our minds.'

So the prophet and the Apostle are in full agreement. God's decisions are truly unfathomable. But once His mouth has made them known, they can also be proclaimed by human lips. What God has spoken man can know. Of the thoughts He has kept secret man can know nothing.

PETER

That is certainly a reasonable solution to the difficulties that I raised. If you know any other miraculous events in this man's life, would you continue with them now?

GREGORY

(17) Under the guidance of Abbot Benedict a nobleman named Theoprobus had embraced monastic life. He was an exemplary religious and had long enjoyed the saint's friendship and confidence. One day on entering Benedict's room he found him weeping bitterly. After he had waited for some time and there was still no end to the abbot's tears, he asked what was causing him such sorrow, for he was not weeping as he usually did at prayer but with deep sighs and lamentation.

'Almighty God has decreed that this entire monastery and everything I have provided for the community shall fall into the hands of the barbarians,' the saint replied. 'It was only with the greatest difficulty that I could prevail upon Him to spare the lives of its members.'

This was the prophecy he made to Theoprobus, and we have seen its fulfillment in the recent destruction of his abbey by the Lombards.[1] They came at night while the community was asleep and plundered the entire monastery without capturing a single monk. In this way God fulfilled His promise to Benedict His faithful servant. He allowed the barbarians to destroy the monastery but safeguarded the lives of the religious. Here you can see how the man of God resembled St. Paul, who had the consolation of seeing everyone with him escape alive from the storm, while the ship and all its cargo were lost.[2]

(18) Exhilaratus, a fellow Roman who, as you know, later became a monk, was once sent by his master to Abbot Benedict with two wooden flasks of wine. He delivered only

---

(17)   [1] Monte Cassino was destroyed by Duke Zotto in 589 and was not rebuilt until 720 under Abbot Petronax.
         [2] Cf. Acts 27.

one of them, however; the other he hid along the way. Benedict, who could observe even what was done in his absence, thanked him for the flask but warned him as he turned to go: 'Son, be sure not to drink from the flask you have hidden away. Tilt it carefully and you will see what is inside.'

Exhilaratus left in shame and confusion and went back to the spot where he had hidden the wine, still wondering what was going to happen. As he tilted the flask a serpent crawled out, and at the sight of it he was filled with horror for his misdeed.

(19)   Not far from the monastery was a village largely inhabited by people the saintly Benedict had converted from the worship of idols and instructed in the true faith. There were nuns living there too, and he used to send one of his monks down to give them spiritual conferences.

After one of these instructions they presented the monk with a few handkerchiefs, which he accepted and hid away in his habit. As soon as he got back to the abbey he received a stern reproof. 'How is it,' the abbot asked him, 'that evil has found its way into your heart?' Taken completely by surprise, the monk did not understand why he was being rebuked, for he had entirely forgotten about the handkerchiefs. 'Was I not present,' the saint continued, 'when you accepted those handkerchiefs from the handmaids of God and hid them away in your habit?' The offender instantly fell at Benedict's feet, confessed his fault and gave up the present he had received.[1]

(20) Once when the saintly abbot was taking his evening meal, a young monk whose father was a high-ranking official[1] happened to be holding the lamp for him. As he stood at the abbot's table the spirit of pride began to stir in his heart. 'Who is this,' he thought to himself, 'that I should have to stand here holding the lamp for him while he is eating? Who am I to be serving him?'

Turning to him at once, Benedict gave the monk a sharp reprimand. 'Brother,' he said, 'sign your heart with the sign of the Cross. What are you saying? Sign your heart!' Then calling the others together, he had one of them take the lamp instead, and told the mur-

---

(19)   [1] Cf. Doyle, *St. Benedict's Rule* 54. 69-70.

(20)   [1] Literally 'a protector'; very likely a 'protector of the municipality' (*defensor civitatis*), the city official who safeguarded the people from exorbitant prices and the dishonesty of private tax collectors. In St. Benedict's time he was one of the most prominent figures in the cities of Italy, a fact which may account for the spirit of pride in this young monk.

murer to sit down by himself and be quiet. Later, when asked what he had done wrong, the monk explained how he had given in to the spirit of pride and silently murmured against the man of God. At this the brethren all realized that nothing could be kept secret from their holy abbot, since he could hear even the unspoken sentiments of the heart.

(21) During a time of famine[1] the severe shortage of food was causing a great deal of suffering in Campania. At Benedict's monastery the entire grain supply had been used up and nearly all the bread was gone as well. In fact, when mealtime came, only five loaves could be found to set before the community. Noticing how downcast they were, the saint gently reproved them for their lack of trust in God and at the same time tried to raise their dejected spirits with a comforting assurance. 'Why are you so depressed at the lack of bread?' he asked. 'What if today there is only a little? Tomorrow you will have more than you need.'

The next day about thirty hundredweights of flour were found in sacks at the gate of the monastery, but no one ever discovered whose services almighty God had employed in bring-

---

(21) [1] Possibly the great famine of 537-38.

ing them there. When they saw what had happened, the monks were filled with gratitude and learned from this miracle that even in their hour of need they must not lose faith in the bountiful goodness of God.

PETER

Are we to believe that the spirit of prophecy remained with the servant of God at all times, or did he receive it only on special occasions?

GREGORY

The spirit of prophecy does not enlighten the minds of the prophets constantly, Peter. We read in Sacred Scripture that the Holy Spirit breathes where He pleases,[2] and we should also realize that He breathes when He pleases. For example, when King David asked whether he could build a temple, the prophet Nathan gave his consent but later had to withdraw it.[3] And Eliseus once found a woman in tears without knowing the reason for her grief. That is why he told his servant who was trying to interfere, 'Let her alone, for her soul is in anguish and the Lord has hidden it from me and has not told me.'[4]

All this reflects God's boundless wisdom and love. By granting these men the spirit of

---

[2] Cf. John 3.8.
[3] Cf. 2 Kings 7.
[4] 4 Kings 4.27.

prophecy He raises their minds high above the world, and by withdrawing it again He safeguards their humility. While the spirit of prophecy is with them they learn what they are by God's mercy. When the spirit leaves them they discover what they are of themselves.

PETER

This convincing argument leaves no room for doubt about the truth of what you say. Please resume your narrative now, if you recall any other incidents in the life of blessed Benedict.

GREGORY

(22) A Catholic layman once asked him to found a monastery on his estate at Terracina.[1] The servant of God readily consented and after selecting several of his monks for this undertaking appointed one of them abbot and another his assistant. Before they left he specified a day on which he would come to show them where to build the chapel, the refectory, a house for guests, and the other buildings they would need. Then he gave them his blessing.

---

(22) [1] A seaport some thirty miles southwest of Monte Cassino.

After their arrival at Terracina they looked forward eagerly to the day he had set for his visit and prepared to receive the monks who might accompany him. Before dawn of the appointed day Benedict appeared in a dream to the new abbot as well as to his prior and showed them exactly where each section of the monastery was to stand. In the morning they told each other what they had seen, but, instead of putting their entire trust in the vision, they kept waiting for the promised visit. When the day passed without any word from Benedict, they returned to him disappointed. 'Father,' they said, 'we were waiting for you to show us where to build, as you assured us you would, but you did not come.'

'What do you mean?' he replied. 'Did I not come as I promised?'

'When?' they asked.

'Did I not appear to both of you in a dream as you slept and indicate where each building was to stand? Go back and build as you were directed in the vision.'

They returned to Terracina filled with wonder and constructed the monastery according to the plans he had revealed to them.

PETER

I wish you would explain how Benedict could possibly travel that distance and then in a vision give these monks directions which they could hear and understand while they were asleep.

GREGORY

What is there in this incident that should raise a doubt in your mind, Peter? Everyone knows that the soul is far more agile than the body. Yet we have it on the authority of Holy Scripture that the prophet Habacuc was lifted from Judea to Chaldea in an instant, so that he might share his dinner with the prophet Daniel, and presently found himself back in Judea again.[2] If Habacuc could cover such a distance in a brief moment to take a meal to his fellow prophet, is it not understandable that Abbot Benedict could go in spirit to his sleeping brethren with the information they required? As the prophet came in body with food for the body, Benedict came in spirit to promote the life of the soul.

PETER

Your words seem to smooth away all my doubts. Could you tell me now what this saint was like in his everyday speech?

GREGORY

(23) There was a trace of the marvelous in nearly everything he said, Peter, and his words

---

[2] Cf. Dan. 14.32-38.

never failed to take effect because his heart
was fixed in God. Even when he uttered a
simple threat that was indefinite and condi-
tional, it was just as decisive as a final ver-
dict.

Some distance from the abbey two women
of noble birth were leading the religious life
in their own home. A God-fearing layman
was kind enough to bring them what they
needed from the outside world. Unfortunate-
ly, as is sometimes the case, their character
stood in sharp contrast to the nobility of their
birth, and they were too conscious of their
former importance to practice true humility
toward others. Even under the restraining
influence of religious life they still had not
learned to control their tongues, and the good
layman who served them so faithfully was
often provoked at their harsh criticisms.
After putting up with their insults for a long
time, he went to blessed Benedict and told
him how inconsiderate they were. The man
of God immediately warned them to curb their
sharp tongues and added that he would have
to excommunicate them if they did not. This
sentence of excommunication was not actually
pronounced, therefore, but only threatened.

A short time afterward the two nuns died
without any sign of amendment and were

buried in their parish church. Whenever Mass
was celebrated, their old nurse, who regularly
made an offering for them, noticed that each
time the deacon announced, 'Everyone who
does not receive Holy Communion must now
leave,' these nuns rose from their tombs and
went outside.[1] This happened repeatedly until one day she recalled the warning Benedict
had given them while they were still alive,
when he threatened to deprive them of communion with the Church if they kept on
speaking so uncharitably.

The grief-stricken nurse had Abbot Benedict informed of what was happening. He
sent her messengers back with an oblation
and said, 'Have this offered up for their souls
during the Holy Sacrifice, and they will be
freed from the sentence of excommunication.'
The offering was made and after that the nuns
were not seen leaving the church any more at
the deacon's dismissal of the non-communi-
cants. Evidently they had been admitted to

---

(23) [1] In the early Church it was customary for the
faithful to receive Communion every time they
assisted at Mass. The deacon's words therefore
applied to the unbaptized and the excommuni-
cated, who were not allowed to remain for the
Mass of the faithful. Their dismissal took place
after the Gospel and sermon.

communion by our blessed Lord in answer to the prayers of His servant Benedict.

PETER

Is it not extraordinary that souls already judged at God's invisible tribunal could be pardoned by a man who was still living in this mortal flesh, however holy and revered he may have been?

GREGORY

What of Peter the apostle? Was he not still living in the flesh when he heard the words, 'Whatever thou shalt bind on earth shall be bound in heaven, and whatever thou shalt loose on earth shall be loosed in heaven'?[2] All those who govern the Church in matters of faith and morals exercise the same power of binding and loosing that he received. In fact, the Creator's very purpose in coming down from heaven to earth was to impart to earthly man this heavenly power. It was when God was made flesh for man's sake that flesh received its undeserved prerogative of sitting in judgment even over spirits. What raised our weakness to these heights was the descent of an almighty God to the depths of our own helplessness.

---

[2] Matt. 16.19.

PETER

Your lofty words are certainly in harmony with these mighty deeds.

GREGORY

(24) One time a young monk who was too attached to his parents left the monastery without asking for the abbot's blessing and went home. No sooner had he arrived there than he died. The day after his burial his body was discovered lying outside the grave. His parents had him buried again but on the following day found the body unburied as before. In their dismay they hurried to the saintly abbot and pleaded with him to forgive the boy for what he had done. Moved by their tears, Benedict gave them a consecrated Host with his own hands. 'When you get back,' he said, 'place this sacred Host upon his breast and bury him once more.'[1] They did so, and thereafter his body remained in the earth without being disturbed again.

---

(24) [1] During the first centuries lay people were permitted to handle the Blessed Sacrament and even keep it in their homes. The practice of placing a consecrated Host on the bodies of those who died in union with the Church was quite common in St. Benedict's time. Cf. A. Rush, *Death and Burial in Christian Antiquity* (Washington 1941) 99-101.

Now, Peter, you can appreciate how pleasing this holy man was in God's sight. Not even the earth would retain the young monk's body until he had been reconciled with blessed Benedict.

PETER

I assure you I do. It is really amazing.

GREGORY

(25) One of Benedict's monks had set his fickle heart on leaving the monastery. Time and again the man of God pointed out how wrong this was and tried to reason with him but without any success. The monk persisted obstinately in his request to be released. Finally Benedict lost patience with him and told him to go.

Hardly had he left the monastery grounds when he noticed to his horror that a dragon with gaping jaws was blocking his way. 'Help! Help!' he cried out, trembling, 'or the dragon will devour me.' His brethren ran to the rescue but could see nothing of the dragon. Still breathless with fright, the monk was only too glad to accompany them back to the abbey. Once safe within its walls, he promised never to leave again. And this time he kept his word, for Benedict's prayers had enabled him to see with his own eyes the in-

visible dragon that had been leading him
astray.[1]

(26) I must tell you now of an event I
heard from the distinguished Anthony. One
of his father's servants had been seized with
a severe case of leprosy. His hair was already
falling out and his skin growing thick and
swollen. The fatal progress of the disease was
unmistakable. In this condition he was sent
to the man of God, who instantly restored
him to his previous state of health.

(27) Benedict's disciple Peregrinus tells of
a Catholic layman who was heavily burdened
with debt and felt that his only hope was to
disclose the full extent of his misfortune to
the man of God. So he went to him and explained that he was being constantly tormented by a creditor to whom he owed seventy dollars.[1]

'I am very sorry,' the saintly abbot replied.
'I do not have that much money in my pos-
session.' Then to comfort the poor man in his
need, he added, 'I cannot give you anything

---

(25) [1] Cf. Apoc. 12.3-9.
(27) [1] Literally 'twelve *solidi*' or gold pieces, amount-
       ing to two ounces of pure gold, nearly a year's
       pay for a skilled workman in the Roman world of
       this period.

today, but come back again the day after to-morrow.'

In the meantime the saint devoted himself to prayer with his accustomed fervor. When the debtor returned, the monks, to their surprise, found thirteen gold pieces lying on top of a chest that was filled with grain. Benedict had the money brought down at once. 'Here, take these,' he told him. 'Use twelve to pay your creditor and keep the thirteenth for yourself.'[2]

I should like to return now to some other events I learned from the saint's four disciples who were mentioned at the beginning of this book.

There was a man who had become so embittered with envy that he tried to kill his rival by secretly poisoning his drink. Though the poison did not prove fatal, it produced horrible blemishes resembling leprosy, which spread over the entire body of the unfortunate victim. In this condition he was brought to the servant of God, who cured the disease with a touch of his hand and sent him home in perfect health.

(28) While Campania was suffering from

---

[2] Cf. 4 Kings 4.7.

famine,[1] the holy abbot distributed the food supplies of his monastery to the needy until there was nothing left in the storeroom but a little oil in a glass vessel. One day when Agapitus, a subdeacon, came to beg for some oil, the man of God ordered the little that remained to be given to him, for he wanted to distribute everything he had to the poor and thus store up riches in heaven.[2]

The cellarer listened to the abbot's command but did not carry it out. After a while Benedict asked him whether he had given Agapitus the oil. 'No,' he replied, 'I did not. If I had, there would be none left for the community.' This angered the man of God, who wanted nothing to remain in the monastery through disobedience, and he told another monk to take the glass with the oil in it and throw it out the window. This time he was obeyed.

Even though it struck against the jagged rocks of the cliff just below the window, the glass remained intact as if it had not been thrown at all. It was still unbroken and none of the oil had spilled. Abbot Benedict had the glass brought back and given to the subdea-

---

(28) [1] The famine mentioned in ch. 21.
      [2] Cf. Luke 18.22.

con. Then he sent for the rest of the community and in their presence rebuked the disobedient monk for his pride and lack of faith.

(29) After that the saint knelt down to pray with his brethren. In the room where they were kneeling there happened to be an empty oil-cask that was covered with a lid. In the course of his prayer the cask gradually filled with oil and the lid started to float on top of it. The next moment the oil was running down the sides of the cask and covering the floor. As soon as he was aware of this, Benedict ended his prayer and the oil stopped flowing. Then turning to the monk who had shown himself disobedient and wanting in confidence, he urged him again to strive to grow in faith and humility.

This wholesome reprimand filled the cellarer with shame. Besides inviting him to trust in God, the saintly abbot had clearly shown by his miracles what marvelous power such trust possesses. In the future who could doubt any of his promises? Had he not in a moment's time replaced the little oil still left in the glass with a cask that was full to overflowing?[1]

(30) One day, on his way to the Chapel

---

(29)   [1] Cf. 3 Kings 17.7-16; 4 Kings 4.1-7.

of St. John at the highest point of the mountain, Benedict met the ancient enemy of mankind disguised as a veterinarian with medicine horn and triple shackle.

'Where are you going?' the saint asked him. 'To your brethren,' he replied with scorn. 'I am bringing them some medicine.'

Benedict continued on his way and after his prayer hurried back. Meanwhile the evil spirit had entered into one of the older monks whom he found drawing water and had thrown him to the ground in a violent convulsion. When the man of God caught sight of this old brother in such torment, he merely struck him on the cheek, and the evil spirit was promptly driven out, never to return.

PETER

I should like to know whether he always obtained these great miracles through fervent prayer. Did he never perform them at will?

GREGORY

It is quite common for those who devoutly cling to God to work miracles in both of these ways, Peter, either through their prayers or by their own power, as circumstances may dictate. Since we read in St. John that 'to as many as received him he gave the power of becoming

sons of God,'[1] why should we be surprised
if those who are the sons of God use this power to work signs and wonders? Holy men can
undoubtedly perform miracles in either of the
ways you mentioned, as is clear from the fact
that St. Peter raised Tabitha to life by praying
over her,[2] and by a simple rebuke brought
death to Ananias and Sapphira for their lies.[3]
Scripture does not say that he prayed for their
death, but only that he reprimanded them for
the crime they had committed. Now, if St.
Peter could restore to life by a prayer and deprive of life by a rebuke, is there any reason
to doubt that the saints can perform miracles
by their own power as well as through their
prayers?

I am now going to consider two instances
in the life of God's faithful servant Benedict.
One of them shows the efficacy of his prayer,
the other the marvelous powers that were his
by God's gift.

(31) In the days of King Totila one of the
Goths, the Arian heretic Zalla, had been per-
secuting devout Catholics everywhere with
the utmost cruelty. No monk or cleric who

---

(30)   [1] John 1.12 (Confraternity Version).
       [2] Cf. Acts 9.36-41.
       [3] Cf. *ibid.* 5.1-10.

fell into his hands ever escaped alive. In his
merciless brutality and greed he was one day
lashing and torturing a farmer whose money
he was after. Unable to bear it any longer,
the poor man tried to save his life by telling
Zalla that all his money was in Abbot Benedict's hands. He only hoped his tormentor
would believe him and put a stop to his brutality. When Zalla heard this, he did stop
beating him but immediately bound his hands
together with a heavy cord. Then, mounting
his horse, he forced the farmer to walk ahead
of him and lead the way to this Benedict who
was keeping his money.

The helpless captive had no choice but to
conduct him to the abbey. When they arrived,
they found the man of God sitting alone in
front of the entrance reading. 'This is the
Abbot Benedict I meant,' he told the infuriated Goth behind him.

Imagining that this holy man could be
frightened as readily as anyone else, Zalla
glared at him with eyes full of hate and
shouted harshly, 'Get up! Do you hear? Get
up and give back the money this man left
with you!' At the sound of this angry voice
the man of God looked up from his reading
and, as he glanced toward Zalla, noticed the
farmer with his hands bound together. The

moment he caught sight of the cord that held them, it fell miraculously to the ground. Human hands could never have unfastened it so quickly.

Stunned at the hidden power that had set his captive free, Zalla fell trembling to his knees and, bending his stubborn, cruel neck at the saint's feet, begged for his prayers. Without rising from his place, Benedict called for his monks and had them take Zalla inside for some food and drink. After that he urged him to give up his heartless cruelty. Zalla went away thoroughly humbled and made no more demands on this farmer who had been freed from his bonds by a mere glance from the man of God.

So you see, Peter, what I said is true. Those who devote themselves wholeheartedly to the service of God can sometimes work miracles by their own power. Blessed Benedict checked the fury of a dreaded Goth without even rising to his feet, and with a mere glance unfastened the heavy cord that bound the hands of an innocent man. The very speed with which he performed this marvel is proof enough that he did it by his own power.

And now, here is a remarkable miracle that was the result of his prayer. (32) One day when he was out working in the fields with

his monks, a farmer came to the monastery
carrying in his arms the lifeless body of his
son. Brokenhearted at his loss, he begged to
see the saintly abbot and, on learning that he
was at work in the fields, left the dead body
at the entrance of the monastery and hurried
off to find him. By then the abbot was already
returning from his work. The moment the
farmer caught sight of him he cried out,
'Give me back my son! Give me back my
son!'

Benedict stopped when he heard this. 'But
I have not taken your son from you, have I?'
he asked.

The boy's father only replied, 'He is dead.
Come! Bring him back to life.'

Deeply grieved at his words, the man of
God turned to his disciples. 'Stand back,
brethren!' he said. 'Stand back! Such a miracle is beyond our power. The holy apostles
are the only ones who can raise the dead.[1]
Why are you so eager to accept what is impossible for us?'

But overwhelming sorrow compelled the
man to keep on pleading. He even declared
with an oath that he would not leave until
Benedict restored his son to life. The saint

---

(32) [1] Cf. Acts 9.36-41; 20.9-10.

then asked him where the body was. 'At the entrance to the monastery,' he answered.

When Benedict arrived there with his monks, he knelt down beside the child's body and bent over it.[2] Then rising, he lifted his hands to heaven in prayer. 'O Lord,' he said, 'do not consider my sins but the faith of this man who is asking to see his son alive again, and restore to this body the soul You have taken from it.'

His prayer was hardly over when the child's whole body began once more to throb with life. No one present there could doubt that this sudden stirring was due to a heavenly intervention. Benedict then took the little boy by the hand and gave him back to his father alive and well.

Obviously, Peter, he did not have the power to work this miracle himself. Otherwise he would not have begged for it prostrate in prayer.

PETER

The way facts bear out your words convinces me that everything you have said is true. Will you please tell me now whether holy men can always carry out their wishes,

---

[2] Cf. *ibid*. 20.10; 3 Kings 17.21.

or at least obtain through prayer whatever they desire?

GREGORY

(33)   Peter, will there ever be a holier man in this world than St. Paul? Yet he prayed three times to the Lord about the sting in his flesh and could not obtain his wish.[1] In this connection I must tell you how the saintly Benedict once had a wish he was unable to fulfill.

His sister Scholastica, who had been consecrated to God in early childhood, used to visit with him once a year. On these occasions he would go down to meet her in a house belonging to the monastery a short distance from the entrance.

For this particular visit he joined her there with a few of his disciples and they spent the whole day singing God's praises and conversing about the spiritual life. When darkness was setting in, they took their meal together and continued their conversation at table until it was quite late. Then the holy nun said to him, 'Please do not leave me tonight, brother. Let us keep on talking about the joys of heaven till morning.'

---

(33)   [1] Cf. 2 Cor. 12.7-9.

'What are you saying, sister?' he replied. 'You know I cannot stay away from the monastery.'

The sky was so clear at the time, there was not a cloud in sight. At her brother's refusal Scholastica folded her hands on the table and rested her head upon them in earnest prayer. When she looked up again, there was a sudden burst of lightning and thunder accompanied by such a downpour that Benedict and his companions were unable to set foot outside the door.

By shedding a flood of tears while she prayed, this holy nun had darkened the cloudless sky with a heavy rain. The storm began as soon as her prayer was over. In fact, the two coincided so closely that the thunder was already resounding as she raised her head from the table. The very instant she ended her prayer the rain poured down.

Realizing that he could not return to the abbey in this terrible storm, Benedict complained bitterly. 'God forgive you, sister!' he said. 'What have you done?'

Scholastica simply answered, 'When I appealed to you, you would not listen to me. So I turned to my God and He heard my prayer. Leave now if you can. Leave me here and go back to your monastery.'

This, of course, he could not do. He had no choice now but to stay, in spite of his unwillingness. They spent the entire night together and both of them derived great profit from the holy thoughts they exchanged about the interior life.

Here you have my reason for saying that this holy man was once unable to obtain what he desired. If we consider his point of view, we can readily see that he wanted the sky to remain as clear as it was when he came down from the monastery. But this wish of his was thwarted by a miracle almighty God performed in answer to a woman's prayer. We need not be surprised that in this instance she proved mightier than her brother; she had been looking forward so long to this visit. Do we not read in St. John that God is love?[2] Surely it is no more than right that her influence was greater than his, since hers was the greater love.

PETER

I find this discussion very enjoyable.

GREGORY

(34) The next morning Scholastica returned to her convent and Benedict to his monastery. Three days later as he stood in

---

[2] Cf. 1 John 4.16.

his room looking up toward the sky, he beheld his sister's soul leaving her body and entering the heavenly court in the form of a dove.

Overjoyed at her eternal glory, he gave thanks to God in hymns of praise. Then, after informing his brethren of her death, he sent some of them to bring her body to the abbey and bury it in the tomb he had prepared for himself. The bodies of these two were now to share a common resting place, just as in life their souls had always been one in God.

(35)   At another time the deacon Servandus came to see the servant of God on one of his regular visits. He was abbot of the monastery in Campania that had been founded by the late senator Liberius, and always welcomed an opportunity to discuss with Benedict the truths of eternity, for he, too, was a man of deep spiritual understanding.   In speaking of their hopes and longings they were able to taste in advance the heavenly food that was not yet fully theirs to enjoy. When it was time to retire for the night, Benedict went to his room on the second floor of the tower,[1] leaving Servandus in the one be-

---

(35)   [1] The watchtower just inside the gate of the ancient fortress; cf. ch. 8 n.10.

low, which was connected with his own by a stairway. Their disciples slept in the large building facing the tower.

Long before the night office began, the man of God was standing at his window, where he watched and prayed while the rest were still asleep. In the dead of night he suddenly beheld a flood of light shining down from above more brilliant than the sun, and with it every trace of darkness cleared away. Another remarkable sight followed. According to his own description, the whole world was gathered up before his eyes in what appeared to be a single ray of light. As he gazed at all this dazzling display, he saw the soul of Germanus, the bishop of Capua, being carried by angels up to heaven in a ball of fire.

Wishing to have someone else witness this great marvel, he called out for Servandus, repeating his name two or three times in a loud voice. As soon as he heard the saint's call, Servandus rushed to the upper room and was just in time to catch a final glimpse of the miraculous light. He remained speechless with wonder as Benedict described everything that had taken place. Then without any delay the man of God instructed the devout Theoprobus to go to Cassino and have a messenger sent to Capua that same night to find out what had happened to Germanus.[2]   In carrying out these instructions the messenger discovered that the revered bishop was already dead. When he asked for further details, he learned that his death had occurred at the very time blessed Benedict saw him carried into heaven.[3]

PETER

What an astounding miracle! I hardly know what to think when I hear you say that he saw the whole world gathered up before his eyes in what appeared to be a single ray of light. I have never had such an experience. How is it possible for anyone to see the whole universe at a glance?

GREGORY

Keep this well in mind, Peter. All creation is bound to appear small to a soul that sees the Creator. Once it beholds a little of His light, it finds all creatures small indeed. The light of holy contemplation enlarges and expands the mind in God until it stands above the world. In fact, the soul that sees Him rises even above itself, and as it is drawn up-

---

[2] Capua is about forty miles southeast of Cassino.

[3] Germanus died in 541; cf. J. Chapman, *St. Benedict and the Sixth Century* (London 1929) 125-26.

ward in His light all its inner powers unfold. Then, when it looks down from above, it sees how small everything really is that was beyond its grasp before.

Now, Peter, how else was it possible for this man to behold the ball of fire and watch the angels on their return to heaven except with light from God? Why should it surprise us, then, that he could see the whole world gathered up before him after this inner light had lifted him so far above the world? Of course, in saying that the world was gathered up before his eyes I do not mean that heaven and earth grew small, but that his spirit was enlarged. Absorbed as he was in God, it was now easy for him to see all that lay beneath God. In the light outside that was shining before his eyes, there was a brightness which reached into his mind and lifted his spirit heavenward, showing him the insignificance of all that lies below.

PETER

My difficulty in understanding you has proved of real benefit, the explanation it led to was so thorough. Now that you have cleared up this problem for me, would you return once more to your account of blessed Benedict's life?

GREGORY

(36) I should like to tell you much more about this saintly abbot, but I am purposely passing over some of his miraculous deeds in my eagerness to take up those of others. There is one more point, however, I want to call to your attention. With all the renown he gained by his numerous miracles, the holy man was no less outstanding for the wisdom of his teaching. He wrote a Rule for Monks that is remarkable for its discretion and its clarity of language. Anyone who wishes to know more about his life and character can discover in his Rule exactly what he was like as an abbot, for his life could not have differed from his teaching.

(37) In the year that was to be his last, the man of God foretold the day of his holy death to a number of his disciples. In mentioning it to some who were with him in the monastery, he bound them to strict secrecy. Some others, however, who were stationed elsewhere he only informed of the special sign they would receive at the time of his death.

Six days before he died he gave orders for his tomb to be opened. Almost immediately he was seized with a violent fever that rapidly wasted his remaining energy. Each day his condition grew worse until finally on the sixth day he had his disciples carry him into the chapel, where he received the Body and Blood of our Lord to gain strength for his approaching end. Then, supporting his weakened body on the arms of his brethren, he stood with his hands raised to heaven and as he prayed breathed his last.[1]

That day two monks, one of them at the monastery, the other some distance away, received the very same revelation. They both saw a magnificent road covered with rich carpeting and glittering with thousands of lights. From his monastery it stretched eastward in a straight line until it reached up into heaven. And there in the brightness stood a man of majestic appearance, who asked them, 'Do you know who passed this way?'

'No,' they replied.

'This,' he told them, 'is the road taken by blessed Benedict, the Lord's beloved, when he went to heaven.'

Thus while the brethren who were with Benedict witnessed his death, those who were absent knew about it through the sign he had promised them. His body was laid to rest in

---

(37) [1] At present the generally accepted date for his death is March 21, 547; cf. ch. 15 n.2.

the Chapel of St. John the Baptist, which he
had built to replace the altar of Apollo.

(38) Even in the cave at Subiaco, where he
had lived before, this holy man still works
numerous miracles for people who turn to him
with faith and confidence. The incident I am
going to relate happened only recently.

A woman who had completely lost her
mind was roaming day and night over hills
and valleys, through forests and fields, resting
only when she was utterly exhausted. One
day in the course of her aimless wanderings
she strayed into the saint's cave and rested
there without the least idea of where she was.
The next morning she woke up entirely cured
and left the cave without even a trace of her
former affliction. After that she remained free
from it for the rest of her life.

PETER

How is it that as a rule even the martyrs in
their care for us do not grant the same great
favors through their bodily remains as they
do through their other relics? We find them
so often performing more outstanding miracles away from their burial places.

GREGORY

There is no doubt, Peter, that the holy
martyrs can perform countless miracles where
their bodies rest. And they do so in behalf of

all who pray there with a pure intention   In places where their bodies do not actually lie buried, however, there is danger that those whose faith is weak may doubt their presence and their power to answer prayers. Consequently, it is in these places that they must perform still greater miracles. But one whose faith in God is strong earns all the more merit by his faith, for he realizes that the martyrs are present to hear his prayers even though their bodies happen to be buried elsewhere.

It was precisely to increase the faith of His disciples that the eternal Truth told them, 'If I do not go, the Advocate will not come to you.'[1] Now certainly the Holy Spirit, the Advocate, is ever proceeding from the Father and the Son.[2] Why, then, should the Son say He will go in order that the Spirit may come, when actually the Spirit never leaves Him? The point is that as long as the disciples could see our Lord in His human flesh they would want to keep on seeing Him with their bodily eyes. With good reason, therefore, did He tell them, 'If I do not go, the Advocate will not come.'[3]   What He really meant was, 'I cannot teach you spiritual love unless I re-

---

(38)   [1] John 16.7 (Confraternity Version).
       [2] Cf. *ibid.* 15.26.
       [3] *Ibid.* 16.7 (Confraternity Version).

move my body from your sight; as long as you continue to see me with your bodily eyes you will never learn to love me spiritually.'

PETER

That is a very satisfying explanation.

GREGORY

Let us interrupt our discussion for a while. If we are going to take up the miracles of other holy men, we shall need a short period of silence to rest our voices.

INDEX